This visitor book belongs to:

MW00453607

....

Dear Visitor,

It's so good to see you.

I'd love you to write a few words

about this visit, to help me

remember it. Thank you!

The next two pages explain how...

Here's half the sample page...

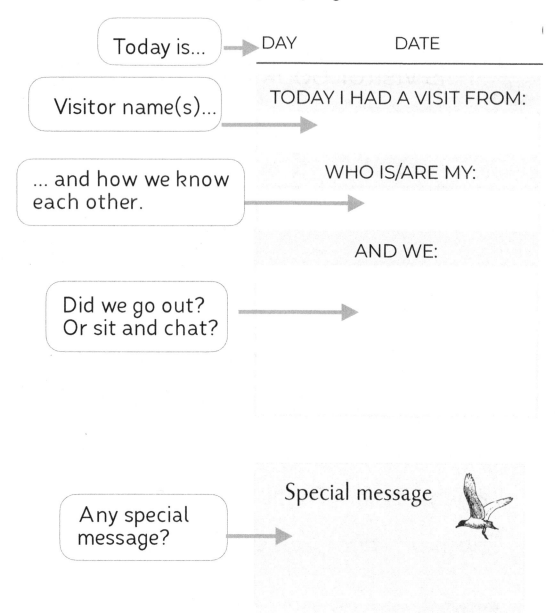

Today is... → DAY   DATE

Visitor name(s)... → TODAY I HAD A VISIT FROM:

... and how we know each other. → WHO IS/ARE MY:

AND WE:

Did we go out? Or sit and chat? →

Any special message? → Special message

Here's the other half...

Visitor BOOK

We talked about...

> This will help me remember...

and about their news...

> ... your visit and your news.

They brought? Took?

> Did you bring anything? A photo, a flower...? Where did you leave it?
>
> Or family, did you take anything away, to clean or repair?

Next visit or contact?

> I'd love to know when I'll see or hear from you next!

Visitor BOOK

DAY   DATE

TODAY I HAD A VISIT FROM:

We talked about...

WHO IS/ARE MY:

AND WE:

and about their news...

Special message

They brought? Took?

Next visit or contact?

Visitor BOOK

TODAY I HAD A VISIT FROM:

We talked about...

WHO IS/ARE MY:

AND WE:

and about their news...

Special message

They brought? Took?

Next visit or contact?

Visitor BOOK

DAY   DATE

TODAY I HAD A VISIT FROM:

We talked about...

WHO IS/ARE MY:

AND WE:

and about their news...

Special message

They brought? Took?

Next visit or contact?

Visitor BOOK

DAY   DATE

TODAY I HAD A VISIT FROM:

WHO IS/ARE MY:

AND WE:

We talked about...

and about their news...

They brought? Took?

Special message

Next visit or contact?

Visitor BOOK

DAY　　　　　DATE

TODAY I HAD A VISIT FROM:

WHO IS/ARE MY:

AND WE:

Special message

We talked about...

and about their news...

They brought? Took?

Next visit or contact?

DAY   DATE

TODAY I HAD A VISIT FROM:

WHO IS/ARE MY:

AND WE:

Special message

We talked about...

and about their news...

They brought? Took?

Next visit or contact?

Visitor BOOK

DAY   DATE

TODAY I HAD A VISIT FROM:

WHO IS/ARE MY:

AND WE:

We talked about...

and about their news...

They brought? Took?

Special message

Next visit or contact?

Visitor BOOK

TODAY I HAD A VISIT FROM:

WHO IS/ARE MY:

AND WE:

Special message

We talked about...

and about their news...

They brought? Took?

Next visit or contact?

Visitor BOOK

DAY   DATE

TODAY I HAD A VISIT FROM:

WHO IS/ARE MY:

AND WE:

Special message

We talked about...

and about their news...

They brought? Took?

Next visit or contact?

Visitor BOOK

DAY   DATE

TODAY I HAD A VISIT FROM:

WHO IS/ARE MY:

AND WE:

Special message

We talked about...

and about their news...

They brought? Took?

Next visit or contact?

Visitor BOOK

DAY   DATE

TODAY I HAD A VISIT FROM:

WHO IS/ARE MY:

AND WE:

We talked about...

and about their news...

They brought? Took?

Next visit or contact?

Special message

DAY   DATE

Visitor BOOK

TODAY I HAD A VISIT FROM:

WHO IS/ARE MY:

AND WE:

Special message

We talked about...

and about their news...

They brought? Took?

Next visit or contact?

Visitor BOOK

DAY   DATE

TODAY I HAD A VISIT FROM:

WHO IS/ARE MY:

AND WE:

Special message

We talked about...

and about their news...

They brought? Took?

Next visit or contact?

Visitor BOOK

DAY   DATE

TODAY I HAD A VISIT FROM:

WHO IS/ARE MY:

AND WE:

Special message

We talked about...

and about their news...

They brought? Took?

Next visit or contact?

Visitor BOOK

DAY   DATE

TODAY I HAD A VISIT FROM:

WHO IS/ARE MY:

AND WE:

Special message

We talked about...

and about their news...

They brought? Took?

Next visit or contact?

Visitor BOOK

TODAY I HAD A VISIT FROM:

WHO IS/ARE MY:

AND WE:

Special message

We talked about...

and about their news...

They brought? Took?

Next visit or contact?

Visitor BOOK

DAY   DATE

TODAY I HAD A VISIT FROM:

We talked about...

WHO IS/ARE MY:

AND WE:

and about their news...

Special message

They brought? Took?

Next visit or contact?

Visitor BOOK

DAY   DATE

TODAY I HAD A VISIT FROM:

WHO IS/ARE MY:

AND WE:

Special message

We talked about...

and about their news...

They brought? Took?

Next visit or contact?

Visitor BOOK

DAY   DATE

TODAY I HAD A VISIT FROM:

WHO IS/ARE MY:

AND WE:

We talked about...

and about their news...

They brought? Took?

Special message

Next visit or contact?

Visitor BOOK

DAY   DATE

TODAY I HAD A VISIT FROM:

WHO IS/ARE MY:

AND WE:

We talked about...

and about their news...

They brought? Took?

Next visit or contact?

Special message

Visitor BOOK

DAY   DATE

TODAY I HAD A VISIT FROM:

WHO IS/ARE MY:

AND WE:

Special message

We talked about...

and about their news...

They brought? Took?

Next visit or contact?

Visitor BOOK

DAY   DATE

TODAY I HAD A VISIT FROM:

WHO IS/ARE MY:

AND WE:

We talked about...

and about their news...

They brought? Took?

Special message

Next visit or contact?

Visitor BOOK

DAY   DATE

TODAY I HAD A VISIT FROM:

WHO IS/ARE MY:

AND WE:

Special message

We talked about...

and about their news...

They brought? Took?

Next visit or contact?

Visitor BOOK

DAY   DATE

TODAY I HAD A VISIT FROM:

WHO IS/ARE MY:

AND WE:

We talked about...

and about their news...

Special message

They brought? Took?

Next visit or contact?

Visitor BOOK

DAY   DATE

TODAY I HAD A VISIT FROM:

WHO IS/ARE MY:

AND WE:

We talked about...

and about their news...

They brought? Took?

Special message

Next visit or contact?

Visitor BOOK

DAY   DATE

TODAY I HAD A VISIT FROM:

WHO IS/ARE MY:

AND WE:

Special message

We talked about...

and about their news...

They brought? Took?

Next visit or contact?

Visitor BOOK

DAY   DATE

TODAY I HAD A VISIT FROM:

WHO IS/ARE MY:

AND WE:

Special message

We talked about...

and about their news...

They brought? Took?

Next visit or contact?

Visitor BOOK

DAY   DATE

TODAY I HAD A VISIT FROM:

WHO IS/ARE MY:

AND WE:

Special message

We talked about...

and about their news...

They brought? Took?

Next visit or contact?

Visitor BOOK

DAY   DATE

TODAY I HAD A VISIT FROM:

WHO IS/ARE MY:

AND WE:

Special message

We talked about...

and about their news...

They brought? Took?

Next visit or contact?

Visitor BOOK

DAY   DATE

TODAY I HAD A VISIT FROM:

WHO IS/ARE MY:

AND WE:

Special message

We talked about...

and about their news...

They brought? Took?

Next visit or contact?

Visitor BOOK

DAY   DATE

TODAY I HAD A VISIT FROM:

WHO IS/ARE MY:

AND WE:

Special message

We talked about...

and about their news...

They brought? Took?

Next visit or contact?

Visitor BOOK

DAY   DATE

TODAY I HAD A VISIT FROM:

WHO IS/ARE MY:

AND WE:

Special message

We talked about...

and about their news...

They brought? Took?

Next visit or contact?

Visitor BOOK

DAY   DATE

TODAY I HAD A VISIT FROM:

WHO IS/ARE MY:

AND WE:

Special message

We talked about...

and about their news...

They brought? Took?

Next visit or contact?

Visitor BOOK

DAY   DATE

TODAY I HAD A VISIT FROM:

WHO IS/ARE MY:

AND WE:

Special message

We talked about...

and about their news...

They brought? Took?

Next visit or contact?

Visitor BOOK

DAY   DATE

TODAY I HAD A VISIT FROM:

WHO IS/ARE MY:

AND WE:

Special message

We talked about...

and about their news...

They brought? Took?

Next visit or contact?

Visitor BOOK

DAY   DATE

TODAY I HAD A VISIT FROM:

WHO IS/ARE MY:

AND WE:

Special message

We talked about...

and about their news...

They brought? Took?

Next visit or contact?

Visitor BOOK

DAY   DATE

TODAY I HAD A VISIT FROM:

WHO IS/ARE MY:

AND WE:

Special message

We talked about...

and about their news...

They brought? Took?

Next visit or contact?

Visitor BOOK

DAY   DATE

TODAY I HAD A VISIT FROM:

WHO IS/ARE MY:

AND WE:

We talked about...

and about their news...

They brought? Took?

Next visit or contact?

Special message

Visitor BOOK

DAY   DATE

TODAY I HAD A VISIT FROM:

We talked about...

WHO IS/ARE MY:

AND WE:

and about their news...

Special message

They brought? Took?

Next visit or contact?

Visitor BOOK

DAY   DATE

TODAY I HAD A VISIT FROM:

WHO IS/ARE MY:

AND WE:

Special message

We talked about...

and about their news...

They brought? Took?

Next visit or contact?

Visitor BOOK

DAY   DATE

TODAY I HAD A VISIT FROM:

We talked about...

WHO IS/ARE MY:

AND WE:

and about their news...

Special message

They brought? Took?

Next visit or contact?

Visitor BOOK

DAY   DATE

TODAY I HAD A VISIT FROM:

WHO IS/ARE MY:

AND WE:

Special message

We talked about...

and about their news...

They brought? Took?

Next visit or contact?

Visitor BOOK

DAY   DATE

TODAY I HAD A VISIT FROM:

WHO IS/ARE MY:

AND WE:

Special message

We talked about...

and about their news...

They brought? Took?

Next visit or contact?

Visitor BOOK

DAY   DATE

TODAY I HAD A VISIT FROM:

WHO IS/ARE MY:

AND WE:

Special message

We talked about...

and about their news...

They brought? Took?

Next visit or contact?

Visitor BOOK

DAY   DATE

TODAY I HAD A VISIT FROM:

WHO IS/ARE MY:

AND WE:

Special message

We talked about...

and about their news...

They brought? Took?

Next visit or contact?

Visitor BOOK

DAY   DATE

TODAY I HAD A VISIT FROM:

WHO IS/ARE MY:

AND WE:

Special message

We talked about...

and about their news...

They brought? Took?

Next visit or contact?

Visitor BOOK

DAY   DATE

TODAY I HAD A VISIT FROM:

WHO IS/ARE MY:

AND WE:

Special message

We talked about...

and about their news...

They brought? Took?

Next visit or contact?

Visitor BOOK

DAY   DATE

TODAY I HAD A VISIT FROM: We talked about...

WHO IS/ARE MY:

AND WE:

                                   and about their news...

Special message

                                   They brought? Took?

                                   Next visit or contact?

Visitor BOOK

DAY   DATE

TODAY I HAD A VISIT FROM:

WHO IS/ARE MY:

AND WE:

Special message

We talked about...

and about their news...

They brought? Took?

Next visit or contact?

Visitor BOOK

DAY   DATE

TODAY I HAD A VISIT FROM:

WHO IS/ARE MY:

AND WE:

Special message

We talked about...

and about their news...

They brought? Took?

Next visit or contact?

Visitor BOOK

DAY   DATE

TODAY I HAD A VISIT FROM:

WHO IS/ARE MY:

AND WE:

Special message

We talked about...

and about their news...

They brought? Took?

Next visit or contact?

Visitor BOOK

DAY   DATE

TODAY I HAD A VISIT FROM:

WHO IS/ARE MY:

AND WE:

We talked about...

and about their news...

They brought? Took?

Next visit or contact?

Special message

Visitor BOOK

DAY   DATE

TODAY I HAD A VISIT FROM:

WHO IS/ARE MY:

AND WE:

Special message

We talked about...

and about their news...

They brought? Took?

Next visit or contact?

Visitor BOOK

DAY   DATE

TODAY I HAD A VISIT FROM:

WHO IS/ARE MY:

AND WE:

We talked about...

and about their news...

They brought? Took?

Special message

Next visit or contact?

Visitor BOOK

DAY   DATE

TODAY I HAD A VISIT FROM: We talked about...

WHO IS/ARE MY:

AND WE: and about their news...

Special message

                                   They brought? Took?

                                   Next visit or contact?

Visitor BOOK

DAY   DATE

TODAY I HAD A VISIT FROM:

WHO IS/ARE MY:

AND WE:

We talked about...

and about their news...

They brought? Took?

Next visit or contact?

Special message

Visitor BOOK

DAY   DATE

TODAY I HAD A VISIT FROM:

WHO IS/ARE MY:

AND WE:

Special message

We talked about...

and about their news...

They brought? Took?

Next visit or contact?

Visitor BOOK

DAY   DATE

TODAY I HAD A VISIT FROM: We talked about...

WHO IS/ARE MY:

AND WE:

and about their news...

Special message

They brought? Took?

Next visit or contact?

Visitor BOOK

DAY   DATE

TODAY I HAD A VISIT FROM:

We talked about...

WHO IS/ARE MY:

AND WE:

and about their news...

Special message

They brought? Took?

Next visit or contact?

DAY   DATE   # Visitor BOOK

TODAY I HAD A VISIT FROM: We talked about...

WHO IS/ARE MY:

AND WE: and about their news...

Special message    They brought? Took?

                                         Next visit or contact?

Visitor BOOK

DAY   DATE

TODAY I HAD A VISIT FROM:

WHO IS/ARE MY:

AND WE:

Special message

We talked about...

and about their news...

They brought? Took?

Next visit or contact?

Visitor BOOK

DAY   DATE

TODAY I HAD A VISIT FROM: We talked about...

WHO IS/ARE MY:

AND WE:

and about their news...

They brought? Took?

Special message

Next visit or contact?

Visitor BOOK

DAY   DATE

TODAY I HAD A VISIT FROM:

WHO IS/ARE MY:

AND WE:

Special message

We talked about...

and about their news...

They brought? Took?

Next visit or contact?

Visitor BOOK

DAY   DATE

TODAY I HAD A VISIT FROM:

WHO IS/ARE MY:

AND WE:

We talked about...

and about their news...

They brought? Took?

Special message

Next visit or contact?

Visitor BOOK

DAY   DATE

TODAY I HAD A VISIT FROM:

WHO IS/ARE MY:

AND WE:

Special message

We talked about...

and about their news...

They brought? Took?

Next visit or contact?

Visitor BOOK

DAY DATE

TODAY I HAD A VISIT FROM:

WHO IS/ARE MY:

AND WE:

Special message

We talked about...

and about their news...

They brought? Took?

Next visit or contact?

Visitor BOOK

DAY   DATE

TODAY I HAD A VISIT FROM:

WHO IS/ARE MY:

AND WE:

We talked about...

and about their news...

They brought? Took?

Next visit or contact?

Special message

Visitor BOOK

DAY   DATE

TODAY I HAD A VISIT FROM:

WHO IS/ARE MY:

AND WE:

Special message

We talked about...

and about their news...

They brought? Took?

Next visit or contact?

Visitor BOOK

DAY   DATE

TODAY I HAD A VISIT FROM:

WHO IS/ARE MY:

AND WE:

Special message

We talked about...

and about their news...

They brought? Took?

Next visit or contact?

Visitor BOOK

DAY   DATE

TODAY I HAD A VISIT FROM:

WHO IS/ARE MY:

AND WE:

We talked about...

and about their news...

They brought? Took?

Next visit or contact?

Special message

Visitor BOOK

DAY   DATE

TODAY I HAD A VISIT FROM:

WHO IS/ARE MY:

AND WE:

Special message

We talked about...

and about their news...

They brought? Took?

Next visit or contact?

Visitor BOOK

DAY   DATE

TODAY I HAD A VISIT FROM:

WHO IS/ARE MY:

AND WE:

We talked about...

and about their news...

They brought? Took?

Next visit or contact?

Special message

Visitor BOOK

DAY   DATE

TODAY I HAD A VISIT FROM:

We talked about...

WHO IS/ARE MY:

AND WE:

and about their news...

Special message

They brought? Took?

Next visit or contact?

Visitor BOOK

DAY   DATE

TODAY I HAD A VISIT FROM:

WHO IS/ARE MY:

AND WE:

Special message

We talked about...

and about their news...

They brought? Took?

Next visit or contact?

Visitor BOOK

DAY   DATE

TODAY I HAD A VISIT FROM:

WHO IS/ARE MY:

AND WE:

We talked about...

and about their news...

They brought? Took?

Next visit or contact?

Special message

Visitor BOOK

DAY   DATE

TODAY I HAD A VISIT FROM: We talked about...

WHO IS/ARE MY:

AND WE:

and about their news...

Special message

They brought? Took?

Next visit or contact?

Visitor BOOK

DAY   DATE

TODAY I HAD A VISIT FROM:

WHO IS/ARE MY:

AND WE:

Special message

We talked about...

and about their news...

They brought? Took?

Next visit or contact?

Visitor BOOK

DAY   DATE

TODAY I HAD A VISIT FROM: We talked about...

WHO IS/ARE MY:

AND WE:

and about their news...

Special message

They brought? Took?

Next visit or contact?

Visitor BOOK

DAY   DATE

TODAY I HAD A VISIT FROM:

WHO IS/ARE MY:

AND WE:

We talked about...

and about their news...

They brought? Took?

Next visit or contact?

Special message

Visitor BOOK

DAY   DATE

TODAY I HAD A VISIT FROM:

WHO IS/ARE MY:

AND WE:

Special message

We talked about...

and about their news...

They brought? Took?

Next visit or contact?

Visitor BOOK

DAY   DATE

TODAY I HAD A VISIT FROM:

WHO IS/ARE MY:

AND WE:

Special message

We talked about...

and about their news...

They brought? Took?

Next visit or contact?

Visitor BOOK

DAY   DATE

TODAY I HAD A VISIT FROM:

WHO IS/ARE MY:

AND WE:

Special message

We talked about...

and about their news...

They brought? Took?

Next visit or contact?

Visitor BOOK

DAY   DATE

TODAY I HAD A VISIT FROM:

WHO IS/ARE MY:

AND WE:

Special message

We talked about...

and about their news...

They brought? Took?

Next visit or contact?

Visitor BOOK

DAY   DATE

TODAY I HAD A VISIT FROM:

WHO IS/ARE MY:

AND WE:

Special message

We talked about...

and about their news...

They brought? Took?

Next visit or contact?

Visitor BOOK

DAY   DATE

TODAY I HAD A VISIT FROM:

WHO IS/ARE MY:

AND WE:

Special message

We talked about...

and about their news...

They brought? Took?

Next visit or contact?

Visitor BOOK

DAY DATE

TODAY I HAD A VISIT FROM:

WHO IS/ARE MY:

AND WE:

Special message

We talked about...

and about their news...

They brought? Took?

Next visit or contact?

Visitor BOOK

DAY   DATE

TODAY I HAD A VISIT FROM:

WHO IS/ARE MY:

AND WE:

Special message

We talked about...

and about their news...

They brought? Took?

Next visit or contact?

Visitor BOOK

DAY   DATE

TODAY I HAD A VISIT FROM:

WHO IS/ARE MY:

AND WE:

Special message

We talked about...

and about their news...

They brought? Took?

Next visit or contact?

Visitor BOOK

DAY   DATE

TODAY I HAD A VISIT FROM:

WHO IS/ARE MY:

AND WE:

Special message

We talked about...

and about their news...

They brought? Took?

Next visit or contact?

Visitor BOOK

DAY   DATE

TODAY I HAD A VISIT FROM:

WHO IS/ARE MY:

AND WE:

Special message

We talked about...

and about their news...

They brought? Took?

Next visit or contact?

Visitor BOOK

DAY   DATE

TODAY I HAD A VISIT FROM:

WHO IS/ARE MY:

AND WE:

Special message

We talked about...

and about their news...

They brought? Took?

Next visit or contact?

Visitor BOOK

DAY   DATE

TODAY I HAD A VISIT FROM:

WHO IS/ARE MY:

AND WE:

Special message

We talked about...

and about their news...

They brought? Took?

Next visit or contact?

Visitor BOOK

DAY   DATE

TODAY I HAD A VISIT FROM:

WHO IS/ARE MY:

AND WE:

Special message

We talked about...

and about their news...

They brought? Took?

Next visit or contact?

Visitor BOOK

DAY   DATE

TODAY I HAD A VISIT FROM:

WHO IS/ARE MY:

AND WE:

We talked about...

and about their news...

They brought? Took?

Next visit or contact?

Special message

Visitor BOOK

DAY   DATE

TODAY I HAD A VISIT FROM:

WHO IS/ARE MY:

AND WE:

Special message

We talked about...

and about their news...

They brought? Took?

Next visit or contact?

Visitor BOOK

DAY   DATE

TODAY I HAD A VISIT FROM:

WHO IS/ARE MY:

AND WE:

Special message

We talked about...

and about their news...

They brought? Took?

Next visit or contact?

Visitor BOOK

DAY   DATE

TODAY I HAD A VISIT FROM:

WHO IS/ARE MY:

AND WE:

Special message

We talked about...

and about their news...

They brought? Took?

Next visit or contact?

Visitor BOOK

DAY   DATE

TODAY I HAD A VISIT FROM:

WHO IS/ARE MY:

AND WE:

Special message

We talked about...

and about their news...

They brought? Took?

Next visit or contact?

Visitor BOOK

DAY   DATE

TODAY I HAD A VISIT FROM:

WHO IS/ARE MY:

AND WE:

Special message

We talked about...

and about their news...

They brought? Took?

Next visit or contact?

Visitor BOOK

DAY   DATE

TODAY I HAD A VISIT FROM:

WHO IS/ARE MY:

AND WE:

Special message

We talked about...

and about their news...

They brought? Took?

Next visit or contact?

Visitor BOOK

DAY   DATE

TODAY I HAD A VISIT FROM:

WHO IS/ARE MY:

AND WE:

Special message

We talked about...

and about their news...

They brought? Took?

Next visit or contact?

Visitor BOOK

DAY   DATE

TODAY I HAD A VISIT FROM:

WHO IS/ARE MY:

AND WE:

Special message

We talked about...

and about their news...

They brought? Took?

Next visit or contact?

Visitor BOOK

DAY   DATE

TODAY I HAD A VISIT FROM:

WHO IS/ARE MY:

AND WE:

We talked about...

and about their news...

Special message

They brought? Took?

Next visit or contact?

Visitor BOOK

DAY　　　　　DATE

TODAY I HAD A VISIT FROM:

WHO IS/ARE MY:

AND WE:

Special message

We talked about...

and about their news...

They brought? Took?

Next visit or contact?

Visitor BOOK

DAY   DATE

TODAY I HAD A VISIT FROM:

WHO IS/ARE MY:

AND WE:

Special message

We talked about...

and about their news...

They brought? Took?

Next visit or contact?

Visitor BOOK

DAY   DATE

TODAY I HAD A VISIT FROM:

WHO IS/ARE MY:

AND WE:

Special message

We talked about...

and about their news...

They brought? Took?

Next visit or contact?

Visitor BOOK

DAY   DATE

TODAY I HAD A VISIT FROM:

WHO IS/ARE MY:

AND WE:

Special message

We talked about...

and about their news...

They brought? Took?

Next visit or contact?

Visitor BOOK

DAY   DATE

TODAY I HAD A VISIT FROM:

WHO IS/ARE MY:

AND WE:

Special message

We talked about...

and about their news...

They brought? Took?

Next visit or contact?

Visitor BOOK

DAY   DATE

TODAY I HAD A VISIT FROM:

WHO IS/ARE MY:

AND WE:

Special message

We talked about...

and about their news...

They brought? Took?

Next visit or contact?

Visitor BOOK

DAY   DATE

TODAY I HAD A VISIT FROM:

WHO IS/ARE MY:

AND WE:

We talked about...

and about their news...

They brought? Took?

Special message

Next visit or contact?

People in my life

NAME	CONTACT

 Thank you for caring!

People in my life

NAME	CONTACT

Thank you for caring!

People in my life

NAME	CONTACT

 Thank you for caring!

People in my life

NAME	CONTACT

Thank you for caring!

Notes

Notes

Wishing you happy times
with your visitors!

Made in United States
North Haven, CT
29 January 2023

31791402R00070